SAINT

Thérèse

OF THE
CHILD JESUS

D1042791

If you'd like to order more copies of this book, please contact:

United States:
America Needs Fatima
(888) 317-5571
P.O. Box 341, Hanover, PA 17331
ANF@ANF.org ▪ www.ANF.org

Canada:
Canada Needs Our Lady
PO Box 36040
Greenfield Park, QC J4V 3N7
844-729-6279
Info@CanadaNeedsOurLady.org ▪ www.CanadaNeedsOurLady.org

© 2018 English Edition
Translation from the original French: Faustine Hillard
Editing: Tonia M. Long
Photography and Design: Felipe Barandiarán and Elizabeth Saracino

ISBN: 978-1-877905-51-3
Library of Congress Control Number: 2018936822

Printed in the United States of America

SAINT Thérèse OF THE CHILD JESUS

FATHER RAYMOND DE THOMAS DE SAINT-LAURENT

CONTENTS

On the day of her canonization, Saint Thérèse of the Child Jesus reaped an incomparable triumph. The Eternal City had seldom seen such an explosion of enthusiasm within its walls. In the morning, the 30,000 pilgrims gathered in the immense Basilica of Saint Peter passionately acclaimed the banner with the smiling face of the young Carmelite. When evening came, the cupola of the Basilica, entirely covered with lights, was resplendent in her honor, and the houses of Rome had been decorated and lit up as a sign of the joy of their inhabitants.

Our dear saint is eminently popular. She is invoked and loved across the globe. She is loved for her gracious, spontaneous, and unpretentious style in recounting her simple life. She is loved for having covered the cross she received as a religious with flowers and caresses while consumed by an implacable illness. She is loved for the beneficial shower of roses she lets fall from Heaven over her

The crowd of 30,000 pilgrims filling Saint Peter's Basilica erupted enthusiastically as the large banner depicting the young Carmelite was brought forward in procession.

innumerable devotees, fulfilling the promise she had made.

Everything about her is attractive and fascinating.

Though her devotees know her, many understand her only imperfectly, and some even hold ideas of her which are in direct contradiction to historical reality. They perceive the radiance of her glory, but they do not penetrate the depths of her soul. They suspect neither the superhuman strength nor the constant heroism that carried this young girl to the highest pinnacles of Christian perfection.

In these few pages we will attempt to revive her true moral features. We wish to accentuate the sanctity of her life, which makes her a true sister of yesterday's giants of virtue, the great saint whom few know how to discover beneath her childish charms.

Saint Thérèse of the Child Jesus

"I would never have believed it possible to suffer so much. Never! Ever! I can only explain it through the ardent desire I have to save souls..."

CHAPTER I

The Thoughtfulness of Grace

Sanctity is the combined work of Divine action and human correspondence, but in this close collaboration, God's part is always the greater. "Without Me, you can do nothing," said Jesus.[1] Therefore, before all else, the soul should abandon itself with docility to the mysterious action of grace. This is the universal law.

This is what happened with little Sister Thérèse. The Most High took possession of her soul; He sculpted, modeled, and embellished it and made of her a masterpiece of celestial beauty.

To achieve the magnificent plan of His most merciful Love, the Divine Majesty made use of two great providential means: suffering and prayer.

* * *

Shortly before her death, Thérèse of the Child Jesus took a certain medicine. Gazing attentively at

---

1. John 15:5.

the glimmer of red liquid in the bottle, she showed it to the religious beside her and said: "This medicine appears to be excellent, but I never knew anything more bitter." Then she added thoughtfully, "This is the precise image of my life; to the eyes of others it always seemed vested in the most joyful colors. They thought I was drinking a delicious liqueur; in reality, it was only bitterness."

Christ, who wanted her entirely for Himself, marked her with the seal of the Cross. From her most tender years, Thérèse was torn by suffering. At the young age of four, she lost her mother. It was a terrible blow. The precocious intelligence of this child fully comprehended the extent of the loss, and her acute sensibility intensified the bleeding wound in her young heart. The sorrow plunged her into a profound silence, a frightening thing when speaking of a child. Her soul was immersed in such an abyss of suffering that she was unable to express her feelings in words. The shock was so violent that the child's disposition changed. Until then Thérèse had been so lively that she was known as the "little ferret," the "little mischief-maker," but now she became excessively sensitive. The slightest emotion

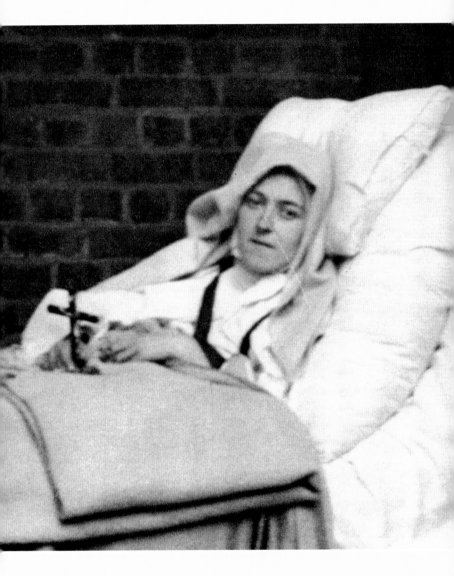

It is through the cross that one attains glory. On her deathbed,
Saint Thérèse of the Child Jesus gave a perfect example of
holiness and taught us that it is precisely when the pain hits us
hardest that we must recognize the loving work of the Most High
in us and salute with joy the dawn of the true light.

The Virgin of the Smile:
"All of a sudden, the Blessed Mother appeared so beautiful that I had never seen anything like it before; her face radiated ineffable goodness and tenderness, but it was her ravishing smile that penetrated my soul to its very depth."

brought tears to her eyes. She fled from the noisy amusements common to children of her age. She felt comfortable only in the warm familial atmosphere where her oldest sister Pauline assumed the role of mother, giving her the prudent and tender affection she needed.

Nevertheless, God soon came to remove this seemingly necessary comfort from this poor little girl. Pauline felt the call from on high to enter the Carmelite order and bravely sacrificed everything to heed it. So it was that even before receiving her first Holy Communion, Thérèse would feel herself twice orphaned.

The "little white flower" felt the wind of the tempest; the fragile stem bent low and there were some who anxiously wondered if she was not going to die. The moral shock so weakened our dear little saint that her health began to fail. She fell gravely ill, languishing for months. When all had already lost hope of saving her, the Most Holy Virgin appeared to her, smiled at her, and miraculously cured her.

Without a doubt, it was a signal grace, but for this child it marked the beginning of a new martyrdom. Her sisters, having seen in her face the signs of the ecstasy,[2] discovered her secret. Their questions obliged her to relate what had happened. By a special disposition of Providence, our dear saint, before crossing the threshold of adolescence, already experienced the threefold suffering that adolescents and religious endure: suffering of the heart, of the body, and of the spirit.

The contradictions and prolonged delays that her vocation encountered left her desolate. But these sufferings did not last long. Thereafter we find her in the Carmel of Lisieux, within the cloister for which she had so thirsted. She confessed that nothing there took her by surprise; she expected the cross, and it was the cross that she found.

She encountered numerous crosses. Some came from her fellow Carmelites. The Superior, a religious of eminent good sense and great firmness,

---

2. Translator's note: The reader will frequently encounter the word "ecstasy" in this work. Regarding this phenomenon, theologians say that it consists of a state of soul in which the senses become disengaged from material things and all that pertains to them. The soul then rises up in contemplation of divine things. This special state is generally found in mystics of contemplative life.

Thérèse *(right)* and her three Carmelite sisters
with their Mother Superior, Mary of Gonzaga
(foreground, left)

soon discovered the treasures in this privileged soul and decided to spur Saint Thérèse's spiritual advancement at a goodly pace. Notwithstanding her tender age, the young nun was treated with a rigid austerity that might have discouraged even the strongest of hearts.

The sisters who shared her daily life appreciated her beautiful natural endowments and sincerely loved her; they did not, however, perceive her sanctity. They came to look upon some of her most generous acts as negligent and imperfect. They considered her a child of great promise, yet still poor in acquired virtues.

But there is more, and here, in order to judge things correctly, it is necessary to admit the will of God. Exquisite charity reigned in Carmel; in accord with the desires of their holy Mother, Saint Teresa of Avila, the sick were given the greatest attention. Now, at the end of Lent, Thérèse suffered a hemoptysis (an expectoration of blood from the respiratory tract) on several occasions. As duty demanded, she did not hide the fact, yet she related it with such gracious simplicity that no one worried about the state of her health. They let her continue her fasting and vigils, unwittingly delaying the treatment her illness required. The Divine Master so desired it, for He wished to harvest this virginal soul speedily for the gardens of His Paradise.

Her crosses in the Carmel of Lisieux were not solely from creatures; some penetrated to the depths of her heart and truly martyred her, for they came from the very hand of God.

What crosses were these that caused her such sorrow?

The first was the trial that befell her family; the father she so tenderly loved grew weak and died after three years of painful agony.

Later came a terrible darkness: frightening temptations against the Faith, incessantly fought but always renewed. Saint Thérèse was tormented for months on end, yet this enormous trial would cease only on her deathbed, when waves of light illuminated the night and, in a great ecstasy of love, Thérèse breathed her last. That we might understand this cruel suffering, we should attentively study the doctrine of Saint John of the Cross concerning passive purification. The limits of this small book do not permit a detailed exposition of this doctrine, but, with unfailing truth, we may affirm that this last spiritual trial of Saint Thérèse surpassed the most painful of natural sufferings.

How radiant she seemed when, in a gesture so recollected and sweet, she pressed bunches of flowers to her crucifix! The roses that filled her hands deliciously perfumed the heart of the Master, serving at the same time to enchant our poor souls, so thirsty for peace and charm.

To us, Thérèse seems enveloped in an atmosphere of poetry and felicity. This is certainly true, though this poetry is the poetry of sacrifice. The roses she holds bloody her fingers and tear at her heart. Because He has loved her, the Most High has treated her as He treated His only begotten Son: "Ought not Christ to have suffered these things, and so to enter into His glory?"[3]

Those who wish to attain sanctity must surrender generously to the action of grace, and God will cause them to ascend the slopes of Calvary. One reaches glory through the cross; there is no other way.

---

3. Luke 24:26.

Thérèse's simple cell in the
Convent of Lisieux.

Many pious people consider themselves on the way to perfection. They have good desires, they savor prayer, and they consider themselves to be soaring in the sublime regions of high virtue. But if sweetness is lacking, if trials arise, they soon become discouraged; they doubt God's tenderness and are tempted to abandon everything.

What a great mistake it is to doubt God! It is precisely when suffering afflicts us that we should recognize the work of the Most High in ourselves and joyously salute the aurora of true light.

To abandon everything: what madness! To turn our backs upon suffering is to turn our backs upon Love and to renounce our sanctification!

* * *

God is infinitely good. In Scriptures we see that His compassion extends even to the irrational animals. He does not subject man, created in His image and likeness, to trials without a reason. When He sends us suffering, it is only to detach us from material goods and persons in order to unite us more closely to Him.

While He granted Thérèse the precious gift of suffering, He united her to Himself through prayer. When she was still a child, a mysterious force led her to seek refuge within herself. She would retire to a corner of the room and remain there, thinking. What did she think about for so long? She knew not how to explain; she felt her soul at ease close to the invisible beings that protected her.

When someone insisted upon knowing the subject of her reflections, she responded, "I am thinking of Heaven." When at times her father took her walking in the countryside, she thought there as well, amid the flowers that were her friends and, I was going to say, her sisters. She thought in like manner at night, gazing at the stars that she so liked to contemplate.

What was the unfamiliar impression that entered little Thérèse's heart on these occasions? It was a clear touch of grace, which, according to the expression of the Holy Books, is the "unction that teacheth all things;"[4] it was the feeling of the presence of God, the very foundation of the grace of prayer.

---

4. 1 John 2:27.

"Our Lord knocking on the door of the heart."
Image painted by Saint Thérèse of the Child Jesus in 1892,
modeled on a similar image in her monastic cell.

Saint Thérèse had already received numerous and profound graces such as these. Later on, she would write with all sincerity that on the day of her First Communion her heart's encounter with Christ was a "fusion of souls." Happy are those who receive such favors! God treats them as friends.

Naturally, these contemplative tendencies would blossom more perfectly when she entered Carmel. Every day she would pray the prayers prescribed by the rule; she would perform all her duties under God's gaze; she would live in an almost uninterrupted union with her most beloved Master.

What were the sentiments she felt in prayer? At times a celestial sweetness filled her heart to overflowing; at other times, there were intense ecstasies, which her fragile body could not long endure without being shattered. But it was aridity, dryness, the "night," to use the language of Saint John of the Cross, that were most frequent. Still, in this dryness was found something profound and substantial that nourished her. This night was not lacking a certain clarity. Upon finishing her prayers, Thérèse would find herself so enlightened that it surprised her.

What does all of this signify? Let us use technical terms. Properly said, it is infused contemplation; it is the habitual "quiet"; it is the frequent "union," the first degree of contemplative perfection; we are in the presence of the summits of ecstasy.

Why all of these explanations, which may seem superfluous? For several significant reasons.

Before all else, it is necessary to vindicate Saint Thérèse in face of certain fumbling admirers who, under the mistaken pretext of making her more "accessible," minimize the gifts she received. These unhappy souls forget that such privileged prayers are not rare. If many do not attain this perfection it is, in the words of Saint Teresa of Avila, much less because God has rejected them than because of their lack of correspondence. It is fitting to recall at this point a truth very little known in our days. When God destines a certain soul to exercise a profound supernatural influence, He raises it up to these states of prayer. Without this assistance it is very difficult to become, in the province of the Church, a first-rate apostle.

Let us, then, safeguard the great lesson the Saint of Lisieux gives us. Prayer is indispensable for attaining sanctity and the exercise of a fruitful apostolate.

"To turn our back on suffering is to turn our back on Love and to renounce our sanctification."

Saint Thérèse of the Child Jesus

Unfortunately, prayer is not duly appreciated. Some see it from afar with a mixture of respect and fear, as if it were an archaeological artifact or a museum piece. Some flee from it, saying that they are incapable of meditation. I realize that this simple spiritual exercise is sometimes made complicated, but is it not quite easy to converse, heart to heart, with the good Master, to remain in His presence like a poor beggar who implores the bread of grace and love?

Others cut their prayers short under the pretext of zeal. This evaluation is erroneous. They lose themselves in sterile activities because they do not know the words of the Savior. They are not entirely united to the grapevine; their branches bear scant fruit. This practical disdain for prayer has, in part, produced the sad century we live in, a century of triumphant mediocrities and disoriented hearts.

* * *

At the time Thérèse of the Child Jesus passed away in Lisieux, the theories known by the name of "Americanism"[5] were beginning to spread. The partisans

5. Translator's note: This was a doctrine promoted by Father Isaac Hecker and widespread at the end of the 19th century, especially in the United States.

of this doctrine wanted a new spirituality for the new times. They ignored that which is the very base of contemplative life; they despised what they disparagingly called the "passive virtues." Pope Leo XIII solemnly condemned these fatal errors.[6]

The years went by, and the Americanists did not manage the conquests they had foretold, nor did they change the face of the world. And behold, the young Carmelite who died in obscurity has attained the summit of glory. By her simple writings she has conquered more hearts for Christ than the most famous preachers with their sermons. She has converted tremendous number of souls. How certain it is that, in order to sanctify oneself and become an apostle, before all else it is necessary to abandon oneself to the action of grace.

---

6. Intending to lead back to the Church those separated from Her, followers of this doctrine proposed that the Church adapt Herself, making concessions in tendencies and principals condemned by the Church. See the encyclical *Testem Benevolentiae* of January 22, 1899.

Thérèse at the age of eight.
(Detail of the photograph on page 35 with her sister Celine)

CHAPTER II

Correspondence to Grace

Since the time she was little, Thérèse had wanted to become a saint. She had always felt a secret certainty that this desire would be fulfilled. She knew, nevertheless, her own weakness; she felt herself to be fragile and small. She was, as she liked to say, but a "little white flower."

How, then, could she, being so fragile, climb the arduous summits of sanctity? Would she renounce her desire for perfection, frightened by such a sizable undertaking? Certainly not. She would surmount this difficulty with her clear good sense.

As she relates in her autobiography, she sought an "elevator" to make up for her weakness. She sought it patiently and with untiring constancy. Finally she recalled the consoling words of the Scriptures: "You shall be carried at the breasts, and upon the knees they shall caress you. As one whom the mother caresseth, so will I comfort you, and you shall be comforted in Jerusalem."[6] Her spirit was illuminated and she exclaimed, "Thine arms, O Jesus, are the elevator by which I will ascend to Heaven!" And she added, "For this, it is not necessary that I grow; on the contrary, I should remain small, even to the point of growing ever smaller."

With this innocent and charming image, Saint Thérèse of the Child Jesus offers us a spiritual doctrine in accord with the highest theology. In order to sanctify ourselves, it is enough that we correspond to grace with perfect docility. Now, the ideal of this correspondence is found in the way of spiritual infancy.

A child is a flower of love. It blooms only in an atmosphere of tenderness; the perfume it emits is nothing but love. A child is innocent, trustful love; simple self-abandoning love.

This is the model chosen by our dear Saint. She would practice "confident love, generous love."

* * *

On the occasion of the great prodigy of the miraculous catch of fish, Peter exclaimed with fright:

---

6. Isaias 66:13.

"Depart from me, for I am a sinful man, O Lord!"[7] Jesus answered smiling, "Fear not."[8] Christ demands our love, but where there is a lack of confidence, love is feeble. In the words of the apostle Saint John, perfect charity eliminates fear: "Perfect charity drives out fear."[9]

If this is true, then Thérèse was outstanding in love, for she lived in absolute confidence. She founded her confidence solely on faith.

She believed that God is an infinitely good Father, who places His unlimited power at the service of His tenderness for us. The beautiful prayer of the "Our Father" enchanted her. At times, the novices found her in her cell with her countenance illuminated by the joy swelling her soul; she was repeating in spirit the touching words of the Lord's prayer.

She believed that Christ is the Divine Friend. She knew about the treasures of charity hidden in His adorable heart. She did not doubt His love even in the severest trials.

---

7. Luke 5:8.
8. Luke 5:10.
9. 1 John 4:18.

The words of the apostle were completely fulfilled in her; she confided blindly in the love God bears us.[10] She knew that everything He sends us, the joys as well as the sorrows, is for our greater good. She received everything from His hand as precious gifts of His infinite tenderness.

Finally, she believed in mercy. Her confidence was not vainly founded on her own merits. She knew that we are nothing in face of unlimited grandeur. She relied solely upon the indescribable compassion of the celestial Father. With the enthusiasm that still vibrates in the pages of her history, she declared it clearly: It was not because she had been preserved from mortal sin that she had so much confidence. She knew the passionate love that Christ has for poor sinners. In the Gospel, we see Him pardon Mary Magdalene and promise His kingdom to the Good Thief. The soul-stirring cry of the Savior resounded in the depths of her heart: "For the Son of Man is come to seek and to save that which was lost."[11] She well knew that our faults, as great as

---

10. 1 John 4:16.
11. Luke 19:10.

Thérèse at the age of eight with her sister Celine.

Thérèse at the age of thirteen.

they may be, are devoured like straw by the divine fire burning in the heart of Christ, no matter how slightly we turn to Him. She also knew that all of us, even the most pure, are creatures. With lively faith and profound humility, she relied on her own destitution to victoriously touch the mercy of God.

Built upon this solid foundation, her confidence was unshakable. Thus, Thérèse felt her soul invaded by that "river of peace" of which Scriptures speak: "Behold I will bring upon her as it were a river of peace."[12]

She did not permit that anything frighten her. What could possibly disturb her? The past, with its faults of old? With good sense, Thérèse observed that God, infinitely just, has our poverty in mind. Moreover, she made of that poverty a motive for confiding.

What could possibly disturb her? The present, at times so laden with suffering and anguish? On the contrary, she recognized in the cross the regal gift of divine Love.

Again, what could possibly disturb her? The

12. Isaias 66:12.

uncertain future, which held for her such sorrowful perspectives? Thérèse lived from day to day, from minute to minute. As she sang in one of her best-known poems, she worked, prayed, and suffered "only for the day at hand." As regards the sufferings of the morrow, she knew that God would send her the help necessary to endure them.

Her confidence expected everything from the celestial Father. She felt immense desires rise up in her soul. She wanted to become a great saint; she wanted to conquer a multitude of souls for God; after her death, she wanted to let fall from Heaven a shower of roses. She confided these desires to Our Lord, and the Master fulfilled them by means of innumerable prodigies.

She also trusted Him to alleviate her sufferings, if He so pleased. Late one afternoon, shortly before her death, the nurse brought her some blankets to help her pass the night. The little saint, consumed by fever, thanked her with a smile; but interiorly, with child-like simplicity, she made known to the Savior the need she had to quench her thirst. And behold, a short time later, and contrary to her routine, the nurse returned with some cool water.

Touched by the solicitous delicacy of the Master, Thérèse wept gratefully.

In an ultimate and splendid manifestation of confidence, Thérèse abandoned herself completely to Providence. In the twilight of her life, she was asked: "Were God to give you the choice of being cured or going to Heaven, what would you do?"

"Oh!" she responded spiritedly, "I would not choose anything."

She possessed true wisdom; she allowed herself to be borne in the arms of God as a little child. Does not Our Lord know what is best for us? Let us not lose the salutary lesson Thérèse of the Child Jesus gives us. Let us anchor our souls on a truly robust faith.

May we have faith in the love of Christ for us. He spilled His precious blood for us to the last drop. After giving evidence of such excessive tenderness, how could He refuse us goods infinitely less than this?

May we have faith in the mercy of the Master. Was it not in order to expiate our sins that He took on flesh like ours, assumed a heart like ours?

May we have faith in these sublime truths in a practical way. In the moment of trial, let us not grumble; let us contemplate with eyes illuminated by the Faith the hand that, for our own good, momentarily mortifies us. After having fallen, let us raise ourselves up promptly, and throw ourselves into His adorable arms, opened wide to welcome us. If only we understood how ardently the Savior desires to clasp us to His heart!

It is vibrant faith in the merciful Love of Jesus that has made the saints.

* * *

True love is confident and generous. False spirituality seeks only the delights of the interior life, and flees from its difficulties. It wants to receive, but refuses to give.

Saint Thérèse of Lisieux gave magnificently. She did not barter with God; she held nothing back. She offered the Most High the most precious of what she had, that which constituted her moral personality. In the dawn of her early infancy, when her reason was scarcely awakened, she gave Him her will. She never took back this magnificent gift. On her deathbed she affirmed that since she was three years old she had never refused the good God

Thérèse at fifteen, shortly before entering the Carmel.

anything. Is this not the very essence of sanctity? Throughout her life she undoubtedly varied the formulas with which she expressed this gift, yet it remained substantially the same.

While still very young, she offered herself to the Child Jesus as if she were a "little ball," that He might play with her as He wished and make use of her according to His adorable will. This gracious image translates itself into the heroic resignation this saint practiced during her life and which she did not restrict merely to words. When her suffering intensified, Thérèse thought that Jesus, in order to amuse Himself, had torn the "little ball," and she considered herself happy for having entertained Him even at this cost. Does one see many children who at ten or twelve years of age practice virtue as solid as this?

Later on, in the prayers of her adolescence, she asked Our Lord not to be irritated with her, promising Him that she would accept everything generously. Some time afterward, she consecrated herself as a victim of holocaust to Merciful Love.

Let the reader not be alarmed at the word "victim." Thérèse was sufficiently humble not to suppose that

God's justice, so offended by the sins of men, could be assuaged by her own merits. She possessed too much good sense to acquaint herself with such "victim souls" as we sometimes meet, souls that groan, always complaining, dissatisfied with everything and everyone except themselves, not understanding that they are frequently the martyrs of their own imagination and cowardice. No, Thérèse's action had nothing like that. She understood the immense desire of the Sacred Heart of Jesus to pour out the adorable love swelling His heart. In order to please Him, she offered Him her soul disengaged of her own free will, that He might dispose of it through His divinely jealous love. She knew that the Lord is a "consuming fire"[13] and that the ineffable martyrdom of charity brought with it terrible sufferings. But even thus far she gave herself; she gave herself entirely. She wanted to live and to die out of love. And how much tenderness she placed on that gift!

It is good to accept the crucifying will of God without complaint, but to accept it with passive

---

13. Deut. 4:24.

resignation is even better. Even this was not enough for Thérèse's generosity; she accepted with joy. She felt that to act in any other way would be a lack of thoughtfulness towards the Lord. If I may dare say so, it is as if God is compelled to send us the trial, but if He does so, it is for our own good. Therefore, Saint Thérèse sought to smile in the face of trials. She fought to succeed perfectly, and she needed time, but in the end, she gained the victory.

She took still another step. To the smile she added a hymn. And the heavier the cross, the more melodious her hymn.

She progressed so marvelously in this way that the trials gladdened her. Let us understand well that this joy is a joy of pure will, which does not suppress the feeling of pain. During her final illness, she was asked: "Why do you seem so content this morning?" to which she responded with all sincerity, "It is because I had two sufferings. Nothing causes me so much joy as do my little sufferings."

Can we comprehend the degree of heroism such resignation entails when practiced for an entire lifetime?

We sometimes find slightly envious souls who question the Divine predilections with a certain bitterness. Why is it, they ask, that a child such as little Thérèse received so many graces and I continue to languish in my tepidity?

Why? First, because God is God. He disposes of His gifts with sovereign liberty. We may add with harsh frankness: Be as generous as was the Saint of Lisieux and God will fill you to overflowing with His favors, as He did her.

Let us give ourselves, then, to the divine Master entirely and without reserve. Let us give Him our intelligence and our will. Let us say to Him that we deliberately and sincerely renounce our own will, in order to lose ourselves in His adorable Will. Let us ask Him to preserve us in this state of offering, for without Him we can do nothing. Above all, let us not revoke our offering.

When a soul seriously fulfills such a resolution, the response of Christ is not long in coming. The soul soon feels itself invaded by divine action, and enters on the way of spiritual progress. It is a fact that experience has proven a thousand times over.

Indeed, is this not the counsel that Jesus gave to

Blessed Angela de Foligno? "I love," He said, "with an immense love the soul that loves Me without deceit."[14]

Is this not the advice of Saint John of the Cross when he declared that it is necessary to lose everything in order to gain everything?

Is this likewise not the counsel of Saint Ignatius, when he caused those participating in his retreats to recite his beautiful prayer: "O Lord, take my will, my liberty, my entire being. Give me only Thy love and Thy grace: with this I am rich enough; I ask nothing more of Thee."

* * *

We will end this chapter with a story of her infancy, described by Saint Thérèse in her autobiographical writings.

When she was still very little, she would climb the staircase of her parents' home, stop on each step, and call, "Mama, Mama!" She would continue to climb only after hearing her mother respond, "Come, my little daughter."

What a marvelous symbol of Thérèse's interior

---

14. *Le Livre des Visions et Instructions de la Bienheureuse Angèle de Foligno*, 6th ed. (Paris: Tralin), p. 69.

life! In every one of her actions she gazed towards the divine Master; she did nothing without the stimulus of His grace, and did everything to please Him.

This is the model we should imitate. Let us remain ever close to the Savior; let us take refuge in His arms in complete abandonment; let us give ourselves over to Him entirely. It is thus that we will follow the method of Thérèse, her way of confidence and love. This "little way" leads to great sanctity; the Church has certified it by canonizing the young Carmelite.

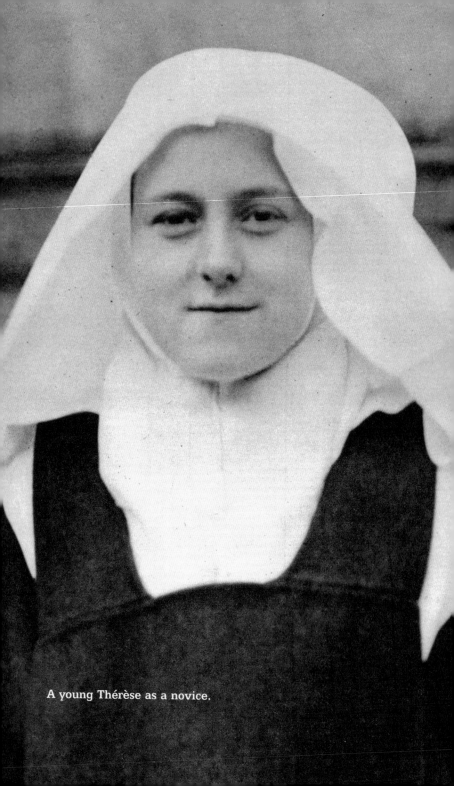

A young Thérèse as a novice.

CHAPTER III

Carmelite Sanctity

An admirable variety reigns among the saints. The virtue of a king, such as Saint Louis IX, is not the same as that of one who becomes a beggar by choice, such as Saint Benedict Joseph Labre. The perfection of an old man, like the great Saint Anthony of the Desert, is not the same as that of a young man like Saint Stanlislaus Kostka. The sanctity of a lay person is not that of a priest or bishop. Each of these sublime heroes of Christian life has his own supernatural countenance.

In this booklet, I intend to study the particular sanctity of little Sister Thérèse. We saw how God formed her soul through suffering and prayer. We saw with what confident and generous love she corresponded to the action of grace in her soul. We must now examine the result of this mysterious collaboration.

Saint John of the Cross (1542-1591)
An example of Carmelite spirituality.

Thérèse's virtue bears the mark of her religious order. Her soul is a privileged flower that blossomed on the heights of Mount Carmel where she fully drank the warm rays of the divine sun. She lived solely for love, and now it is the inebriating perfume of love that she exudes. Our dear Saint is a true daughter of Saint John of the Cross and of Saint Teresa of Avila.

* * *

In our days, how little known is the great Saint John of the Cross, mystical writer, so methodical, clear, and profound! How poorly understood he is! Many are turned aside and isolate themselves from him because of strange preconceptions; they dare not attempt to read his works, looking upon them from a distance with a kind of superstitious fear. They prefer insipid authors who make the piety of the faithful anemic.

Thérèse of the Child Jesus did not fall into this error. A true Carmelite, she read the writings of that great saint, loved them, and made of them, after the Gospel, her principal nourishment. She knew them so well that one could say she knew them by heart, and she quotes them frequently. When her superiors commanded her to write the story of her life, entire passages and verses from the "Spiritual Canticle" flowed from her pen.

Thérèse did not content herself merely with studying the doctrine of Saint John of the Cross; she lived it or, to put it precisely, it lived in her.

It is absolutely necessary at this point that we summarize this doctrine, for we cannot understand Sister Thérèse's supernatural demeanor perfectly without it.

Saint John of the Cross begins with a solid principle that serves as the basis for his doctrine. The perfect union of the soul with God—the mystical love that is a fusion of hearts—occurs only in a pure and completely disinterested faith. The Holy Ghost assures us of this in Sacred Scripture, saying to the privileged soul, "I will espouse thee to me in faith."[15]

Are the conclusions derived from this principle not already evident? If pure faith alone unites us to God in the contemplative embrace, to attain this end it is evidently necessary to renounce everything

---

15. Hosea 2:19.

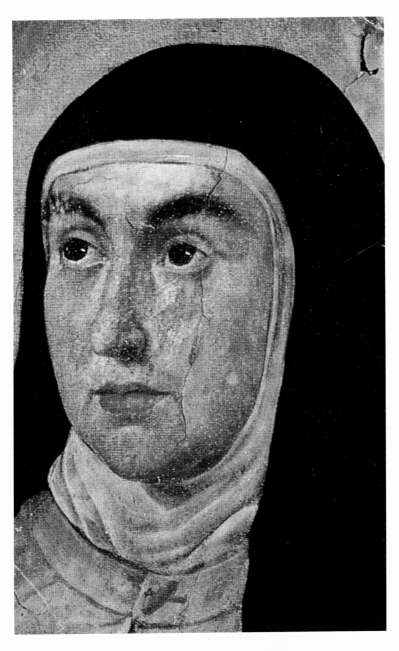

Saint Teresa of Avila (1515-1582)
Referred to today as "The Big Flower."

**Sister Thérèse of the Child Jesus surrounded by the novices,
including her sister Celine, with Mothers Mary of Gonzaga and
Agnes of Jesus (Pauline) in the background.**

that is not this faith. According to the expression of Saint John of the Cross, it is necessary to "go calling out," to go calling for the well-beloved Master, to withdraw from creatures and from oneself. Therefore, the soul that thirsts for divine union should first, by its own efforts and the assistance of grace, rid itself of any natural pursuit, of any attachment no matter how small, and of any spirit of property. It must purify and mortify its interior movements, emptying itself of all that is not of God.

But this first operation realized by the soul is not enough. It is necessary that the Lord intervene directly in a very special manner. It is necessary that by means of sorrowful aridity God free the soul from its habitual manner of prayer. It is absolutely necessary that He force the soul to disengage itself from its imagination and sensibility. Since God is simple and infinite, He cannot communicate Himself to us perfectly by means of sensible forms. Finally, it is necessary that, by means of a dim and desolate flame, God root out all bad inclinations.

Everything here should reassure those timorous spirits who are frightened by Saint John of the Cross. Our holy author does not risk exciting the unhealthy imaginations of certain persons. On the contrary, he professes an enormous suspicion regarding the imagination. If he has high esteem for infused and obscure contemplation, he flees with a kind of terror from interior words, visions, and private revelations. These extraordinary favors pass through sensible forms, and are consequently subject to illusion. He greatly prefers simpler prayer in which the soul, recollected and lost in the presence of God, is inflamed with a most ardent love for God.

The soul penetrates into the profound prayer of which we spoke in the first chapter in the measure that these active and passive purifications progress. It receives in succession the favors of recollection, quiet, and union. It ascends even more if the divine Master calls it to the dizzying heights of ecstasy and spiritual matrimony, which not all Saints attain.

We have summarized as briefly as possible the essential aspects of the doctrine of Saint John of the Cross.

Thérèse of the Child Jesus understood this doctrine marvelously. Once a novice confided her interior dispositions to her. This novice, finding herself

*"All my hopes
have been fulfilled."*

still far from her goal, exclaimed in her generous ardor, "How far I have yet to go!"

Our saint replied vividly, "Oh! Above all say, 'How much I have yet to lose!'"

Indeed, to penetrate the divine mystery it is necessary to lose everything including ourselves.

Thérèse of the Child Jesus practiced this doctrine, ridding herself of everything.

She mortified her flesh by means of fasts, vigils, and austerities.

She mortified her curiosity. One night she felt a hot regurgitation reach her lips. She was elated, knowing that it might announce the approach of death, but she waited until morning to verify that it was blood that had reddened her handkerchief.

She mortified her imagination. A religious once showed her a figure of some angels dressed in white and with palms in their hands, to which she responded smiling: "These images do me no good; I feed myself only with truth."

She mortified her sensibility. For many years in the Carmel she constantly worked alongside the sister who in times past had served as her mother. Yet, she never committed a fault against silence, nor did she ever take advantage of these encounters to manifest her tenderness and open her heart to her sister.

As Saint John of the Cross wished, she truly withdrew from herself; she "went out calling" to the divine Master: "Reveal Thy presence, and may Thy sight and Thy kindness make me die."[16] God responded to the appeal of His privileged daughter. He purified her in the "night," in aridity, in trials, and in the terrible temptation against the Faith. Afterwards, He caused her to penetrate into the depths of prayer, of which we treated earlier.

On the way to sanctity, Thérèse of the Child Jesus climbed, one by one, all the steps described by Saint John of the Cross. She is his true spiritual daughter, in all the strength of the expression.

* * *

She is also a true daughter of the great Saint Teresa of Avila. The Carmelites of Lisieux call attention to this particular fact: The portraits drawn by the contemporary biographers of the illustrious reformer apply in almost every detail to Saint Thérèse. I do not

---

16. *Spiritual Canticle,* Saint John of the Cross.

concern myself with whether or not these two saints resembled one another physically, but I do know that there is a striking similarity between their two souls.

Teresa of Avila is the "Saint of Love." Who was consumed with more ardent charity? An angel pierced her heart with a fiery dart; the evidence of this wound can be clearly seen even today in her miraculously incorrupt heart.

From whom did the fire of divine passion at times elicit more sublime and vibrant cries? One may read the "Exclamations," which burst from her soul after she had received Holy Communion. Hastily written as notes then, today they fill us with admiration.

Who lived with Christ in more profound intimacy? Jesus raised her up to Himself, took her as His spouse, desired that their spirits merge in a mysterious union. Teresa of Avila conversed with the divine Master in respectful familiarity. On a day of a particularly painful trial, Our Lord said to her, "This is how I treat My friends." The Saint responded with trusting boldness, "It does not surprise me, Lord, that Thou hast so few!" Christ felt an infinitely touching kindness toward His servant. The reformer's great

...hérèse depicted ...g images of the ...evotions which ...passed the ...ty of her ...ality and which ...dded to her name ...igion: the Child ...and the Holy Face.

Holy card of the Child Jesus which
Saint Thérèse carried in her breviary.

work was once in danger of collapse; powerful ene-
mies implacably sought to ruin her. Desolate, Saint
Teresa felt her strength wane. But Jesus appeared to
her; He encouraged her; He sweetly obliged her to
take nourishment; His condescension went so far
that He broke the bread Himself and handed it to
her. He rekindled her ardor and communicated to
her an indomitable energy.

Whose actions gave better evidence of the intensi-
ty of their love? The Saint of Avila lived only for God.
She divided her time in two parts; one was consecrated to prayer, the other to arduous work that surpasses our imagination. She traversed Spain and covered
it with monasteries. She built houses; took charge of
numerous affairs; maintained an immense correspondence, writing to bishops, to princes, to the King.
Nothing deterred the impetus of her zeal, because an
overflowing charity inspired it. All of this did not pre-
vent her from dedicating entire hours every day to the
most elevated contemplation. This holy Mother is the
"Saint of Love" par excellence.

Like her, Thérèse of the Child Jesus is also a saint
of love. She understood that the Church is an organ-
ized body. It has a head, which is its Chief; it has

arms, which work in the apostolate. Thérèse of Lisieux eagerly desired to become the heart of the Church. Her vocation was to love: to love only Christ, fully and passionately.

She permitted her love to flow into her writings. She expressed particularly moving exclamations wherein we recognize the echo of those given forth in times past by the virgin of Avila. She proved this love by the generosity of her virtue. She would like to have proven it even by working in a pagan land for the salvation of souls. When preparations to establish a Carmel in Saigon were underway, she was one of the first to offer herself for this distant foundation.

Teresa of Avila is the "Saint of the Apostolate." If she reformed the Order of Carmel, was it not for rekindling the flame of zeal, for reviving the fire that consumed the ancient prophets? She lamented the sad devastations wrought by heresies in those days. She wanted her daughters to become, by prayer, efficient cooperators with the clergy, a thought that frequently appears in her writings.

Saint Thérèse felt herself moved by the same zeal. Her thoughts continually turned towards the heroic missionaries who preached the Gospel to the infidels.

The sisters in the convent laundry.

Harvesting hay in the monastic enclosure.

At the end of her life, she had been ordered to walk every day in the garden of the convent. She obeyed punctually; but she walked with such difficulty that a religious counselled her to desist from this exercise. "No, no," she replied, "with my sufferings I hope to obtain some relief for the poor missionaries so weakened by fatigue that they drag themselves painfully throughout those distant lands."

Teresa of Avila is the "Saint of Common Sense." With what clarity and vivacity she warned her daughters concerning bad judgment! If the reforming Saint had a maternal heart, she also possessed a manly intelligence; she did not hesitate to delicately poke fun at little feminine caprices. Here with a smile, there with a firm word, she repressed the affectations of humility and poorly considered sacrifices. One sister, under the pretext of recollection, complained about joining recreation on a great feast day; Teresa reprimanded her severely and gave her a penance.

There exists in the writings of Teresa of Avila a page that delights me. One chapter of *The Way of Perfection* ends with an exclamation that marvelously reveals the spontaneity of her good sense: "From foolish devotions, free us, O Lord!" What would the great Saint say were she to come across certain writings of dull piety which circulate in our days? What would she think of certain printed religious images? One such example depicts the Sacred Heart encircled by a crown of forget-me-nots with a symbolic dove above it. The artist did not dare paint the heart red, but a bland rose color, the color of a lady's room, of an anemic little girl. Is this not a parody of the sublime and infinite truth? Is this not to be ignorant of the infinite Love, the immeasurable charity that took Christ to Calvary and made Him spill his Blood for us, even to the last drop?

Thérèse of Lisieux was likewise a saint of good sense. She showed herself inflexible in face of certain extravagances. One of the novices had a little tearful devotion. Saint Thérèse urged her to collect her tears in a seashell, as if they were precious pearls. The cure was prompt and radical.

Thérèse judged things soundly. She kept her opinions to herself, but she also expressed them with all simplicity if her superiors so requested. Thus it was that on her deathbed she revealed what she thought about certain austerities. There are penances, she said, which are possible in Spain but

By her example, Saint Thérèse demonstrates
that all effective apostolate is fueled
by an intense and deep interior life.

become harmful when practiced in other climates; it is necessary to take the latitudes into account. Upon reflecting how these long-practiced penances might have shaken the little saint's health, we simultaneously admire her clear discernment and her courage in enduring so much.

* * *

Thérèse of the Child Jesus lived the life of Carmel with heroic perfection. She merited, therefore, an ideal death.

In *The Living Flame of Love*, the most sublime of his works, Saint John of the Cross describes the death of true contemplatives. It is, he said, accompanied by a marvelous elegance. They die in admirable ecstasies. Their final canticle, like that of the swan, is the most melodious.

The great Teresa of Avila died like this. She entered into ecstasy. The sister who attended her, Anna of Saint Bartholomew, saw Christ Himself envelop her soul, after which Teresa's soul flew to Heaven.

The death of the dear Saint of Lisieux happened likewise. The ecstasy illuminated and transfigured her face. Afterwards, her body sank; the soul had freed itself in its final transport.

Photograph of Saint Thérèse taken shortly after her death.

CHAPTER IV

The Shower of Roses

What a contrast between the anonymity in which Saint Thérèse lived and the glory shining over her tomb today! The world, which she abandoned while still young, did not know her. In her convent, the religious loved her for her kindness and good disposition—she was always smiling. But many did not imagine the treasures hidden in her soul. When Thérèse was agonizing, a young sister asked loudly: "Our little Sister of the Child Jesus is enchanting, but she never did anything admirable. What can we tell of her in her biographical notice?"

The Saint died, and her radiant figure captivates hearts. The number of her admirers grows incessantly. Her reputation extends beyond the borders of France. The multitude of those devoted to her is recruited everywhere: from Europe, from the most distant regions, as far as the mission countries. When the Sovereign Pontiff elevated her to the honor of the altars, the Catholic world trembled with immense joy. All this because Thérèse bears the aura of the wonder workers on her brow. The power of her intercession is so marvelous that one rarely finds a similar avalanche of miracles in the history of the saints.

From the heights of Heaven, Thérèse clearly exercises a beneficent mission. A curious thing—and here her prophetic spirit is clearly apparent—is that she foresaw this mission and announced it many times prior to her death.

During one of her last evenings on this earth, she said, "I feel that my mission is going to begin, my mission to make God loved as I love Him...of giving my little way to souls." The angelic child added words that so contributed to popularize her memory: "I wish to pass my Heaven doing good on earth." In other circumstances she declared, "After my death I will let fall a shower of roses." To a religious who was saddened by her departure and asked her to watch over her from the heights of Heaven, she responded, "I will come down."

She herself confessed that an interior voice consoled her. The saints encouraged her saying: "While you are still enfettered, you cannot fulfill your mission; but later, after you have died, your time of conquests will be fulfilled."

Thérèse was not deceived. Events confirmed these prophecies. Thérèse let fall from Heaven a marvelous shower of roses. Everywhere, the miracles attributed to her intercession followed one another without ceasing.

First, there were the temporal favors. Thérèse is actively occupied with her devotees. She cures their illnesses when the doctors have lost all hope. She resolves the most complicated affairs, effects unheard-of prodigies. In favor of an afflicted Carmelite, she multiplied the bank notes in a sealed envelope. Throughout the wars, she demonstrated her powerful protection. She saved some from grave dangers; for others, against all expectations, she obtained the precious aid of the Sacraments.

But above all, she granted spiritual favors. How many impressive conversions her prayers obtained! It seems as if Our Lord refuses nothing to the one who so loved Him while on earth. Some Protestants reading the story of her life felt inspired; a sweet and mysterious force opened

Saint Thérèse's parents *(above)*, Zélie and Louis Martin.

"Les Buissonnets" in Lisieux *(below)*, where
Mr. Martin moved his family after the death of his wife.

A gauche, l'ancien Palais Épiscopal XIIe et XIIIe siècles, actuellement Palais de Justice.

LISIEUX — Cathédrale Saint-Pierre, XIIe sie

Lisieux in 1873, with the Cathedral of Saint Peter in the background

Commemorative stamp issued by Vatican City on the occasion of the centenary of the saint's birth in 1873. It depicts the Martin family home in Alençon where Thérèse was born.

their eyes and led them to the truth. In the mission countries, pagans felt moved to embrace the Faith while gazing upon her printed image.

Thérèse did not forget the Catholics. She managed to lead them to the long-neglected practice of their religious duties; she shook off their torpor and transformed their lamentable tepidity into fervent charity. She gave peace to all, that delightful peace that surpasses all sentiments. In the past she awed her companions with the charm of her smile; now, she sends us her smile from Heaven.

But that is not all. Point by point, the Saint fulfilled all of her promises; she "came down!" More than once she appeared surrounded by a silver light and caused the sound of her voice to be heard. With even greater frequency, without showing her glory, she made her presence felt by means of perfumes unknown on earth, in which the fragrances of roses and incense intermingled. That these prodigious and well-corroborated manifestations continue is itself a rare, if not unique, phenomenon.

Perhaps the most surprising aspect of the miracles of our Saint, one which demonstrates their supernatural origin, is their clearly apostolic character. What she dreamed of during her life came to be after her death: Thérèse became a great converter of souls.

Providence thus gives us a lesson of the greatest importance, and how much we need it! In our days, even the best are frequently victims of a deplorable error. They confuse action with agitation. While moved by an indisputable zeal, they want to do good, but in their works they include that trembling note so characteristic of our era; they seem to rely more on their natural action than on divine grace. Is the cause of our few successes, not to mention our failures, not to be found in this practice?

May we have the courage to face the truth. Whatever their fecundity, our "works," although very numerous, never seem to give the fruits corresponding to the immense efforts we make. It is because we too often forget the teachings of the Faith and of history.

What does the Faith tell us? By ourselves, we can do nothing; we haven't the capacity to convert a single soul, to move a single heart. The help of grace is absolutely necessary. We are but little instruments in the hands of God. The apostle well understood this,

writing to the Corinthians: "I have planted, Appolos watered; but God gave the increase."[17] Because God is jealous of His glory, He desires that every apostolic success be attributed to Him: "But we have this treasure in earthen vessels, that the excellency may be of the power of God, and not of us."[18]

What does history teach us? The great apostles were great contemplatives. John the Baptist drew the multitudes to the banks of the Jordan, but in the desert he led a life of prodigious recollection and penance. The apostles transformed the world, but when the material side of the ministry absorbed them, they established the diaconate. For themselves, after having prayed at length, they reserved the mission of preaching. Saint Vincent de Paul is the man of action par excellence of modern times, but in the midst of weighty occupations and without losing his interior peace, he found a way to spend several hours before the Blessed Sacrament every day. The holy Cure of Ars attended more than one hundred thousand penitents a

17. 1 Cor. 3:6.
18. 2 Cor. 4:7.

Page of Thérèse's autobiography in which she recounts her healing on May 13, 1883.

year, but his life, wholly dedicated to God, was an uninterrupted prayer.

Shall I cite other examples when before our eyes we have Jesus, the Divine Model? The Savior consecrated thirty years of His earthly life to contemplation, but dedicated only three to His public life. Even in those three years of public life, while preaching during the day, at night He retired to the hills to pray.

In confiding an apostolic mission to Thérèse, did the Most High not wish to call our attention to the necessity of the interior life? To accomplish His work, He chose a young daughter, a cloistered religious, a contemplative, who preferred an act of renunciation to the great manifestations admired by the multitudes.

O Saint Thérèse of the Child Jesus, make us imitate thee! Obtain for us abundant graces of the interior life so that our apostolate might become, like thine, irresistibly efficacious.

* * *

The "little flower" of Lisieux is a great miracle-worker.

Let us now pose a question, perhaps an audacious

one, and seek to delve a bit into the impenetrable designs of the Most High. Why is Our Lord pleased to perform so many prodigies through the intercession of His young servant?

By nature, a miracle is a sign. It manifests celestial intervention in an unequivocal manner. It is by miracles that God lends credence to the extraordinary missionaries He sends to men. When He wishes to sanction His doctrine, He recognizes it with the dazzling signature of a miracle. To the evil Pharisees, who obstinately denied His Messianic character, Our Lord countered with His miracles: "The works themselves, which I, do give testimony of me, that the Father hath sent me."[19]

Now, the doctrine of our saint is very precise. During her life, she explained it to the novices, adorning it with the refreshing colors of her gracious imagination. Now, from on high, she calls us to follow her "little way," which led to such glory. This doctrine is summarized in two words: love and confidence.

We were made to love: this is our end, the end

---

19. John 5:36.

Altar of Our Lady of Victories in Paris. It was at the foot of this statue that Thérèse felt assured that it was indeed the Mother of God who had smiled and cured her.

for which we were created. To act only for love is to conquer Heaven at a swift pace and by means of a shorter way. There is nothing painful about this way; there is nothing easier, nothing more delightful, than to love. Christ, in whom resides the plenitude of the Divinity, possesses all the victorious attractions of His adorable attributes and His holy humanity. Let us allow ourselves to be conquered by His infinite charms. Let us give our wills over to Him entirely and without reserve. Let us open wide to Him the portal of our hearts; He will inundate them with graces and form them with His divine hands.

Let us seek to please Him in everything. "It is necessary," Thérèse used to say, "to conquer Jesus with caresses, and to cast at His feet the flowers of small sacrifices." In a word, to forget ourselves, to think only of Him, act only for Him, lose ourselves in Him. And to do so with love, confidence.

The divine Master is adorably good. His tenderness desires only the best for us. What, therefore, could disturb us?

The future? But the overflowing charity of Jesus prepares it. Let us abandon ourselves blindly into

His arms, as a child in the arms of its father.

The past? But our imperfections, even our faults, do not repel Him from us, provided that we are sincerely sorry for having offended Him and recognize that we can do nothing without Him.

The present? At times it bears contradictions, pain, and anguish. But these trials are the regal tokens of infinite Love. May we know how to receive them with a smile upon our lips, with a canticle of recognition in the depths of our hearts.

Confidence such as this opens to us the treasures of divine generosity; we will be attended in the measure of our hope.

There are persons, versed in the spiritual sciences, who do not perceive the admirable profundity of this doctrine. They glance superficially upon the writings of the young Carmelite and smile with a mixture of pity and irony. In them they see naught save the gracious devotion of a young maiden! They do not allow themselves to be conquered by the strength of her words; they do not perceive in those poetic forms the substance of a Saint Paul or a Saint John of the Cross. They do not tremble with joy at seeing the sublime doctrine of love through annihilation of oneself adorned with alluring colors. How odd, these wise ones! They smile at this profound doctrine and prefer those second-rate devotions in which spiritual progress consists of scrupulous calculations written on little scraps of paper.

For the good of souls, it was necessary that this state of things change. God intervened and confirmed this doctrine with innumerable miracles.

Therefore, let us fearlessly follow the little way of Thérèse. This way is certain. The saint solemnly confirmed it to an Italian Carmelite in one of her most famous apparitions.

This way is swift. It leads us quickly to true perfection.

How beautiful our lives would become, how fruitful our efforts would be, what peace would enter our souls, were we to abandon ourselves without reserve to the Most Merciful Love of Jesus Christ!

* * *

In ending this brief study, let us ask Saint Thérèse of the Child Jesus to let fall abundantly over us her beneficent "shower." Let us ask of her the temporal favors we most need. Let us ask of her, above all, supernatural graces, the roses of divine Love.

An act of perfect charity is more useful to the Church than some ostentatious work done without love. Thérèse now carries out the conquest of the world because she was a contemplative and her heart burned with love.

Saint Thérèse of the Child Jesus, grant that we may understand and live for Love. Thou who art so powerful and so good, obtain even this favor for us, which our bold misery implores: after having lived solely for love, grant that one day we might die in it.

Novena to Saint Thérèse of the Child Jesus

Start the Novena with this prayer each day:

Dearest Saint Thérèse of the Child Jesus, you said that you would spend your time in heaven doing good on earth.

Your trust in God was complete. Pray that He may increase my trust in His goodness and mercy as I ask for the following petitions... *(mention your intentions)*

Pray for me that I, like you, may have great and innocent confidence in the loving promises of our God. Pray that I may live my life in union with God's plan for me, and one day see the Face of God whom you loved so deeply.

Saint Thérèse, you were faithful to God up until the moment of your death. Pray for me that I may be faithful to our loving God. May my life bring peace and love to the world through faithful endurance of love for God our savior. *Amen.*

DAY ONE

Loving God, you blessed Saint Thérèse with a capacity for a great love. Help me to believe in your unconditional love for each of your children, especially for me.

Saint Thérèse, privileged Little Flower of Jesus and Mary, I approach you with childlike confidence and deep humility.

I lay before you my desires, and beg that through your intercession they may be realized.

Did you not promise to spend your heaven doing good upon earth? Grant me according to this promise the favors I am asking from you.

Our Father... Hail Mary... Glory Be...

DAY TWO

Loving God, you loved Saint Thérèse's complete trust in your care. Help me to rely on your providential care in each circumstance of my life, especially the most difficult and stressful.

O dear little Saint Thérèse, as I am one of those children for whom Christ died, obtain for me all the graces I need in order to profit by that Precious Blood.

Use your great power with our divine Lord and pray for me.

Our Father... Hail Mary... Glory Be...

DAY THREE

Loving God, you gave Saint Thérèse the ability to see You in the ordinary routine of each day. Help me to be aware of your presence in the everyday events of my life.

Dear Little Flower, make all things lead me to heaven and God. Whether I look at the sun, the moon, the stars and the vast expanse in which they float, or whether I look at the flowers of the field, the trees of the forest, the beauties of the earth so full of color and so glorious, may they speak to me of the love and power of God; may they all sing His praises in my ear.

Like you may I daily love Him more and more in return for His gifts. Teach me often to deny myself in my dealings with others, that I may offer to Jesus many little sacrifices.

Our Father... Hail Mary... Glory Be...

DAY FOUR

Loving God, You taught Saint Thérèse how to find You through the "little way" of humility and simplicity. Grant that I may never miss the grace hidden in humble service to others.

Dear Little Flower of Carmel, bearing so patiently the disappointments and delays allowed by God, and preserving in the depths of your soul an unchanging peace because you sought only God's will, obtain for me a complete conformity to that adorable Will in all the trials and disappointments of life.

If the favors I am asking during this Novena are pleasing to God, obtain them for me. If not, it is true I shall feel the refusal keenly, but I wish only God's Will as you did. I pray that Jesus will be the perfect fulfillment of all my wishes as He was for you.

Our Father... Hail Mary... Glory Be...

DAY FIVE

Loving God, You gave Saint Thérèse the gift of forgiving others even when she felt hurt and betrayed. Help me to be able to forgive others who have wounded me, especially...

Little Flower of Jesus, from the very first moment of your religious life you thought only of denying yourself in all things so as to follow Jesus more perfectly; help me to bear patiently the trials of my daily life.

Teach me to make use of the trials, the sufferings, the humiliations, that come my way, to learn to know myself better and to love God more.

Our Father... Hail Mary... Glory Be...

DAY SIX

Loving God, Saint Thérèse experienced every day as a gift from You. She saw it as a time to love You through other people. May I, too, see every day as an opportunity to say yes to You.

Saint Thérèse, Patroness of the Missions, be a great missionary throughout the world to the end of time. Remind our Master of His own words, "The harvest is great, but the laborers are few."

Your zeal for souls was so great, obtain a like zeal for those now working for souls, and beg God to multiply their numbers, that the millions to whom Jesus is yet unknown may be brought to know, love and follow Him.

Our Father... Hail Mary... Glory Be...

DAY SEVEN

Loving God, Saint Thérèse offered to You her weakness. Help me to see in my weakness an opportunity to rely completely on you.

O little martyr of Love, you know now even better than in the days of your pilgrimage that Love embraces all vocations; that it is Love alone which counts, which unites us perfectly to God and conforms our will with His. All you sought on earth was love; to love Jesus as He had never yet been loved.

Use your power in heaven to make us love Him. If only we love Him we shall desire to make Him loved by others; we shall pray much for souls. We shall no longer fear death, for it will unite us to Him forever.

Obtain for us the grace to do all for the love of God, to give Him pleasure, to love Him so well that He may be pleased with us as He was with you.

Our Father... Hail Mary... Glory Be...

DAY EIGHT

Loving God, You loved Saint Thérèse with a powerful love and made her a source of strength to those who had lost faith in You.

Help me to pray with confidence for those in my life who do not believe they can be loved.

Dear Saint Thérèse, like you I have to die one day. I beseech you, obtain from God, by reminding Him of your own precious death, that I may have a holy death, strengthened by the Sacraments of the Church, entirely resigned to the most holy Will of God, and burning with love for Him.

May my last words on earth be, "My God. I love You."

Our Father... Hail Mary... Glory Be...

DAY NINE

Loving God, Saint Thérèse never doubted that her life had meaning. Help me to see how I can bless and love everyone in my life.

Dear Little Saint Thérèse, by love and suffering while you were on earth, you won the power with God which you now enjoy in heaven. Since your life there began, you have showered down countless blessings on this poor world; you have been an instrument made use of by your divine Spouse to work countless miracles.

I beg of you to remember all my wants. Sufferings must come to me also, may I use them to love God more, and follow my Jesus better. You are especially the little missionary of love.

Make me love Jesus more, and all others for His sake. With all my heart I thank the most Holy Trinity for the wonderful blessings conferred on you, and upon the world through you.

Our Father... Hail Mary... Glory Be...